INTRODUCTION

From the streets of Argentina to becoming the best player on the planet, the story of Lionel Messi is a footballing fairytale.

Messi's story proves that it doesn't matter how big or strong you are, or how rich your parents are, or where you were born. Anything is possible if you are good enough and you work hard enough.

Messi has always had a special talent. That was obvious from an early age when he grabbed every chance he could to improve his skills, and soon the older boys were struggling to get the ball off him.

That has been the story all the way through Messi's life as helpless defenders struggle to stop him. When Messi is at his best, nobody can stop him. The number

of goals he has scored and trophies he has won prove that.

Even a medical problem which stopped him from growing properly as a child has not held Messi back. Barcelona were so keen to sign him that they paid for the injections which helped him grow and they have been rewarded in style.

It is why Messi will always be grateful to his club. Barcelona were the ones that helped to turn his dream into reality as he made Spain his new home. The move to Europe could not have worked out much better. Messi has already won a crazy number of trophies and broken an unbelievable amount of records, both for himself and for his team. And the best thing is, he still has time to win much more!

Children now want to be him, every player wants to be on the same team as him, and managers would all love to sign him.

Perfect role model

The success has not gone to his head either. Despite everything he has won, Messi remains modest about how good he is. It is not just his skill which is a shining example to everyone. His behaviour and his attitude make Messi the perfect role model.

The striker has not forgotten his roots too. He had the chance to play for Spain but Messi is proud to be from Argentina and said he could not imagine playing for any other country. He has many qualities to admire and loyalty is one of them.

Football may never see another player quite like Messi. He is a true football superstar.

EARLY YEARS

The little boy who became the world's greatest footballer was born in a modest area and needed medicine to help him grow. When Barcelona paid for his treatment, his future was sealed...

Lionel Andres Messi was born on June 24, 1987 in Rosario, Argentina. It was a time when Diego Maradona was the big superstar in the South American country. Around one year before Messi was born, Maradona had been captain of the national team that won the World Cup in Mexico.

He possessed many of the same skills as Messi has now and he was able to slalom past defenders like they weren't there. Many believed he was the greatest player there had ever been, along with Pele of Brazil.

Just 12 months after Maradona inspired Argentina's success at Mexico '86, a new star was born.

Messi was the youngest of three brothers for parents Jorge, a steel factory worker, and Celia, a cleaner, while he also has a younger sister.

He lived in what he describes as "a nice, ordinary house" which his family still own. Having received his first ball when he was around four years old, he started playing with his older brothers and cousins.

The house did not have a garden, so Messi would enjoy kickabouts in the street outside his home in the run-down area in which they lived. It was not long before he joined neighbourhood side Grandoli, where father Jorge was involved in the coaching and most of his family played at different levels. It was already clear his son was a very special talent as other boys struggled to get the ball off him.

A shy and humble Messi kicked a ball at every opportunity outside the school classroom. At the age of eight, he went on to join the youth system of local professional side Newell's Old Boys. It was a club which Maradona had not long left as his own career was drawing to an end.

Expensive injections

However, just as obvious as his outstanding ability, it was becoming ever more apparent that Messi was smaller than most other boys. Around a year or so later the doctors discovered he had a restrictive growth hormone deficiency, meaning he was not growing as much as he should.

The expensive injections to help him grow were paid for at first but all that later changed. Messi's family were left with huge costs to pay for his continued treatment. Newell's Old Boys were unable to afford the bill and Argentina giants River Plate – a big club who were watching Messi – did not want to pay either.

In 2000, when he was 13 years old, Barcelona came into Messi's life to start a journey that would take him to the very top of the game. He was invited to

"It wasn't difficult for me to move to Barcelona because I knew I had to. I needed money for my medicine to help me grow and Barcelona were the only club that offered."

Little Lionel feels the cold in a paddling pool with his two older brothers.

Spain for a 15-day trial and very quickly made an impression on Barca technical director Carles Rexach. He had nothing else to use so, incredibly, he agreed to sign Messi and pay for his medical bills in a contract which was written out on a paper napkin!

Messi and his father returned to Argentina where the rest of the family started packing their bags to leave South America for Barcelona, just as Maradona had done himself back in 1982.

"It wasn't difficult for me to move to Barcelona because I knew I had to," Messi said. "I needed money for my medicine to help me grow and Barcelona were the only club that offered. So as soon as they did, I knew I had to go."

The little four-year-old Messi (standing, second right) was soon showing off his skills with local children's team Grandoli in his home city of Rosario. Below, he is second right in the front row two years later.

SUPER-CAMPEONA CAT. 87 "A"

MAKING OF A GENIUS

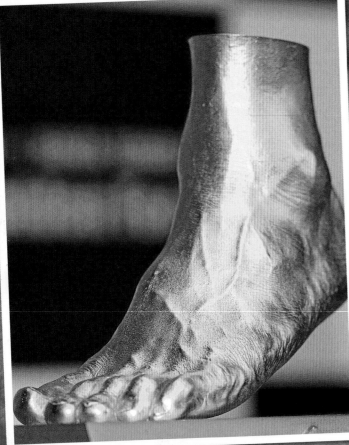

ATTITUDE
Often seen with a smile on his face and humble about his record-breaking achievements, Messi simply loves playing football. And he nearly always does so in the right way with 100 per cent commitment, honesty and loyalty.

RESPONSIBILITY
Being the leading player on the planet is a heavy burden to carry but it does not seem to affect Messi, who rarely produces anything less than his world-class best week in, week out.

LOW CENTRE OF GRAVITY
Perfect example of how smaller players can use their size to their advantage. With superb balance and great lower-body strength, Messi is able to ride tackles, weave his way through the smallest of gaps and change direction in a flash to leave opponents bamboozled.

THE WIZARD'S WAND
It often looks as if the ball is glued to Messi's left foot, such is his brilliant dribbling and control. It is also a deadly weapon when it comes to shooting. Messi is equally capable of smashing home a screamer from long range as he is delicately chipping a helpless goalkeeper. A gold cast of Messi's left foot went on sale in Tokyo for more than £3.4 million.

INTELLIGENCE

Messi's razor-sharp brain, combined with his natural talent and instinct, make him the ultimate attacking machine. He is ultra-cool when in goalscoring positions, rarely wasting any opportunity to find the back of the net, while he is also just as good at creating goals for team-mates with his awesome passing.

DETERMINATION

Messi was told he would not make it as a professional footballer as a youngster, but never gave up his dreams and has proved the doubters and critics wrong in spectacular fashion.

PACE

He is deceptively quick and his tremendous acceleration from the second he picks up the ball allows him to speed past defenders before they have a chance to react. Messi has admitted that being smaller has forced him to become faster, and there are few who can keep up with him when he is in full flight.

SPANISH ADVENTURE

Although small in stature, Messi did not take long to make a big impression at Barcelona after moving to Spain with his family.

Starting at the Spanish club's famous La Masia training academy – a sort of Hogwarts for talented young footballers – Messi's raw natural ability was clear to see.

However, it was not all plain sailing for the quiet and shy young South American in his first few years in Europe.

Messi had all the normal problems of trying to adapt to a new life in a new country. He suffered an ankle injury in his first season too, which ruled him out for a while. A delay in getting registered properly also delayed him being able to play competitive matches for Barcelona.

Swift and spectacular

He finally received his playing licence from the Catalan Football Federation on March 6, 2001, and Barcelona wasted no time in giving him a chance to show what he could do, handing him his debut with the boys' team just 24 hours later. Wearing the number nine shirt, those watching that day in the match against Amposta would have seen something that would become as regular as clockwork in the years that followed – a Messi goal and a Barcelona win.

Messi's rise after that was swift and spectacular. As he grew in size and improved his stamina, Messi was increasingly able to show what he could do. He made his way up through the various youth ranks at Barcelona in lightning-quick fashion as he quickly proved himself good enough for the level above.

Josep Boada, one of Messi's first coaches at Barca, recalled: "He had an extra gear. If the top gear was fifth, he could find a sixth, and that meant at some times he was unstoppable."

Messi was initially played wide out left in the Barcelona youth teams but he kept drifting into the middle. He was looking to become a playmaker who controlled matches and scored goals, like his idol Diego Maradona.

It was a playing style Barcelona fans have now become well accustomed to. After his rapid progress through Barcelona's youth teams on the back of

Messi (front, second left) lines up with the Barcelona youth team. Also in the picture are Gerard Pique (back, fifth left) and Cesc Fabregas (back, third right) who would go on to become senior colleagues.

"He was small and skinny, but when he had the ball at his feet he had a tremendously competitive spirit."

an avalanche of goals, Messi soon found himself representing the club at Under-19 level despite still being much younger.

Pere Gratacos, who was in charge of Barcelona's B side between 2003 and 2005, said of the young Messi: "He was an extraordinary player. He did things with ease, making difficult things look easy, and he did this regularly, it wasn't by chance. He was sensational.

"Physically he couldn't bring anything to the team. He was small and skinny, but when he had the ball at his feet he had a tremendously competitive spirit."

Then, still only 16 and yet to even feature for the club's reserve side, Messi was given his chance to play for Barcelona's first team.

Fine performance

Frank Rijkaard, Barca's head coach, was looking for squad players to boost numbers for a friendly against Porto in November 2003 and Messi – on Gratacos' recommendation – was one of those chosen by the Dutchman.

Messi only played the last quarter-of-an-hour of the match against the Portuguese side but proved he was not out of his depth at that level with a fine performance.

Following his brief taste of first-team action, Messi then returned to Barcelona's reserve side to continue improving his skills while at the same time joining up with the senior squad for training sessions on an increasing basis.

Then, in October 2004, at the age of 17, Rijkaard deemed Messi ready to make his competitive debut for Barcelona in the derby against Espanyol – marking the start of what has become a legendary career.

THE BIG TIME

Messi may have been smaller in height than many of his opponents growing up at Barcelona but he was head and shoulders above them in terms of talent.

The question that still had to be answered was whether Messi could make the massive step up to first-team football? He would now be playing against men much older, much bigger and much more experienced than him. Could he fulfil the remarkable promise he had been showing since he was a kid in Argentina? The answer to those questions has been a definite yes.

Such was his potential that Barcelona had no problems making Messi the second youngest player ever to appear for their first team when he took the field in the local derby against Espanyol.

Seven months later Messi earned himself another place in Barcelona history by becoming the club's youngest ever goalscorer. He achieved that against Albacete on May 1, 2005, when he picked up a scooped pass from Brazil star Ronaldinho before coolly lobbing the keeper. The Messi goal

machine was up and running, and the record books were about to take a hammering.

As the months passed, Messi became stronger, more settled among the first-team superstars at Barca, and with it his influence started to grow. In his first season he played a small role as Barcelona became Spanish champions for the first time since 1999. He became more important the following year, 2006, as he helped the 'Blaugrana' retain their league title and also reach the final of the Champions League.

Lengthy injury

That was the first time Barcelona had got to the European final since 1994 but although they lifted the trophy with victory over Arsenal, Messi was left out of the matchday squad. That was a huge disappointment for the Argentinian, who had been fit for the final after recovering from a lengthy injury.

But, like in all good stories, there were always going to be setbacks and disappointments along the way. Injuries were a major frustration for Messi as his career developed, especially problems with his hamstrings. He was also criticised after punching the ball into the net during Barcelona's derby against Espanyol in 2007 – and getting away with it! That is not something Messi will look back on with pride, unlike two other games around the same time which showed the very best of him.

Still only a teenager, Messi proved there was something very special about him when he scored

continued on page 16

Celebrating becoming Barca's youngest ever goalscorer, against Albacete in 2005.

Messi celebrates his first hat-trick by kissing the Barcelona shirt – and it was against deadly rivals Real Madrid.

The Club World Cup made it an incredible six competitions out of six for Barcelona in 2009.

continued from page 14

a stunning hat-trick for Barca against their arch-rivals Real Madrid in a 3-3 draw. A month later, he then netted what could go down as the greatest goal of his career. It came against Getafe in a Copa del Rey (Spanish Cup) match and saw him run from inside his own half, beating half the opposition defence and also the keeper before scoring.

Messi continued to go from strength to strength in the following seasons, but while his star was on the rise, things were not going quite so well for Barcelona as a team. From being champions of Europe and Spain in 2006, they suddenly found themselves without a single trophy for the next two years.

It was a team on the decline, but that was all about to change when Pep Guardiola replaced Frank Rijkaard as head coach in the summer of 2008. Guardiola, the former Barcelona captain who had also come up through the youth ranks, decided changes were needed. One of the biggest changes was allowing Ronaldinho – voted as the best player in the world in 2004 and 2005 – to leave and give his coveted number 10 shirt to Messi, who had previously worn number 19. It was a huge honour and show of faith by Guardiola in the young Argentinian... and Messi did not let him down.

With the likes of Andres Iniesta and Xavi helping to get the very best out of Messi, Barcelona enjoyed the most successful period in their history as they won an astonishing 14 trophies in just four seasons under Guardiola. The highlight was in 2009 when they won all six tournaments they entered – the Primera Division, Champions League, Copa del Rey, Spanish Supercup, European Supercup and Club World Cup.

Swamped with silverware

Messi played crucial roles in all those successes and as Barca found themselves swamped with silverware, he was finally recognised as the best player on the planet when he won the Ballon d'Or award for the first time in 2009. Most worrying for his rivals, Messi insisted in 2010 that there was still more to come from him.

"I don't think I've reached my peak yet. My aim is to keep improving day by day. I want to keep on growing (as a player)," he said.

And he was proved absolutely right, going on to dominate the FIFA Ballon d'Or awards in the subsequent years and firmly establishing himself as not only the best player in the world, but possibly the best player of all time.

Messi wore the number 19 shirt when he first made it into the Barcelona team, but he inherited the famous number 10 when Brazil star Ronaldinho left the club.

And in 2009 he was to succeed double winner Ronaldinho as world player of the year for the first time – and show off his fashion sense!

YOUTH CLUB

With his career at Barcelona quickly gathering pace,
Messi announced himself on the world stage in the
2005 FIFA World Youth Championship.

 Argentina had to get past Germany and
Spain on their way to the final of Messi's
first tournament at world level.

Messi had made his Under-20 debut for
Argentina in a friendly the year before
but was still to make his full debut for his
country's senior team.

He was selected in his nation's squad
to compete at the 2005 FIFA World Youth
Championship, later called the Under-20 World
Cup, which was taking place in Holland – and it
was there that Messi made people outside Spain
and Argentina really sit up and take notice.

However, the tournament could not have got
off to a much worse start as coach Francisco
Ferraro's side lost 1-0 to the United States. Messi
started on the bench – alongside teenage striker
Sergio Aguero – and was sent on at the start of
the second half, but it made no difference.

Argentina's second group game was against
Egypt and, with Messi this time starting, he
opened the scoring with his first goal of the
competition just after half-time. Captain Pablo
Zabaleta – later to star for Manchester City with
Aguero – then added a second goal late on to
secure a 2-0 victory.

Mazy runs

A 1-0 victory over Germany came next, although
Messi failed to score and was subbed late in the
game. That result meant Argentina finished
second in their group and were through to the
knockout stages.

Messi, already catching the eye with his fast,
mazy runs and close ball control, produced his
second goal of the tournament in a 2-1 win over
Colombia in the second round. He won the ball
himself, played a one-two as he burst into the area,
escaped a challenge and fired home.

In the quarter-finals, Argentina met a Spain
side boasting the likes of Cesc Fabregas and
David Silva but again they proved too strong and

Messi scores from the spot in the final against Nigeria and celebrates his first honour at international level.

triumphed 3-1. Messi netted the third goal of the tournament with a well-taken finish – just one day after his 18th birthday. Not a bad present!

And so it was Brazil, Argentina's great rivals, who lay in wait in the semi-finals. Messi showed no fear as he opened the scoring early on in a dramatic 2-1 win, picking up the ball 25 yards out, taking a couple of touches inside and firing into the top corner for his fourth goal.

Golden Boot

Messi had inspired his nation to reach the final, where they would meet Nigeria, and he was not about to stop there. Shortly before half-time he picked up the ball near the halfway line and set

off on a trademark run which eventually saw him fouled in the area. He picked himself up and slotted home the resulting penalty.

Nigeria had no answer to Messi and he was upended again in the 75th minute before once more sending the goalkeeper the wrong way from the penalty spot to clinch a 2-1 victory – Argentina were the Under-20 World Cup champions for a fifth time.

It was Messi's first honour at international level while his six goals earned him the Golden Boot and his performances secured the Golden Ball which was awarded to the star player, an accolade Argentina legend Diego Maradona himself won back in 1979.

EL CHAMPION

A glittering array of superstars have contributed to Barcelona's domination over recent years, including the likes of Ronaldinho, Samuel Eto'o, Xavi and Andres Iniesta, but the stand-out performer has undoubtedly been Messi.

Barcelona were without a Primera Division title in five years when Messi made his first-team debut in 2004, but in the subsequent nine seasons the Catalan giants finished as top dogs in Spain on six occasions.

The first of those came in the 2004/05 season, although the young Messi only had a small hand in that success with one goal from eight appearances, most of them as a substitute.

He made a much bigger contribution the following year as Barcelona retained their title in emphatic fashion, finishing 12 points clear of their nearest rivals Real Madrid. That season Messi struck six times in 17 league games, and would almost certainly have got many more goals but for an injury that sidelined him for the final few months of the season.

Barcelona were then beaten to the title by Madrid for the next two seasons, despite Messi becoming an increasingly dominant force in the game with a series of superb performances.

After going two years without winning any competition, Barcelona decided to replace head coach Frank Rijkaard with Pep Guardiola in the summer of 2008. That marked the start of the greatest period in the club's history – with Messi central to their record-breaking success.

In the next three years, Barcelona would claim trophy after trophy, including three successive Primera Division titles.

In the 2008/09 season, they finished nine points clear of second-placed Real Madrid in a campaign which saw them score an incredible 105 goals. Messi grabbed 23 of them in 31 appearances.

Hottest property

The following season Messi scored 34 goals in 35 matches as Barca retained their title with a 99-point haul, losing just once in 38 games all season. Messi finished as the leading scorer in both the Primera Division and in Europe for the first time in his career, as well as equalling the club-record 34 goals Ronaldo scored for Barcelona in 1996/97.

Messi was now firmly established as the hottest property in the game and he was back among the goals in 2010/11 as Barcelona claimed a hat-trick of league titles.

The Argentinian found the back of the net 31 times in 33 league games, although he was outscored by Real

Messi gets a champagne shower from team-mate Gerard Pique as they celebrate the 2008/09 title.

Madrid superstar Cristiano Ronaldo, who scored 40 goals that season.

All things must come to an end however, and although Messi himself was in record-breaking goalscoring form during the 2011/12 season, Barcelona were unable to win a fourth successive league title. Jose Mourinho's Real Madrid took their crown after becoming the first team in the history of La Liga to reach 100 points in a single campaign.

Messi was simply phenomenal that season though, breaking Spanish and European records as he finished with a mind-boggling 50 goals in 37 league matches.

Madrid only had the Primera Division title for one year before the trophy was heading back to the Nou Camp. Barcelona – now under new coach Tito Vilanova following the departure of Guardiola in the summer of 2012 – won the 2012/13 campaign with Messi again leading the charge.

Messi was still in his own half when he started to twist and turn past Getafe defenders...

...Messi looks seriously pleased with himself as he celebrates one of the greatest goals of his career...

"It was really special to score a goal like that, and I don't know if I'll ever be able to repeat it. It's a moment I'll never forget."

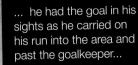

... he had the goal in his sights as he carried on his run into the area and past the goalkeeper...

...and eventually his amazed team-mates catch up with him to join in the celebrations of an incredible moment.

BARCELONA 5 GETAFE 2

Spanish Copa del Rey
April 18, 2007

Messi has scored many memorable goals for club and country, but his amazing strike against Getafe in the Spanish Cup will take some beating.

Diego Maradona's famous second goal for Argentina in the 1986 World Cup quarter-final win over England is considered by many to be possibly the best goal of all time, and Messi produced an almost identical effort for Barcelona 21 years later.

Picking up the ball five metres inside his own half the twinkle-toed magician skipped past two opposing defenders as he raced over the halfway line, and accelerated towards the edge of the Getafe box, where he evaded two more desperate attempts to stop him. There was still work to do but Messi was not to be denied his wonder goal, cleverly rounding the goalkeeper before neatly dinking a right-footed shot over a sliding defender on the line.

23

THAT'S A FACT 1

Nov 16 2003
Makes first-team debut in a friendly at Porto, aged 16.

May 1 2005
Becomes youngest player to score for Barcelona in La Liga with his goal against Albacete.

Dec 1, 2009
Scores winning goal in extra time to earn Barcelona their first Club World Cup title with a 2-1 win over Estudiantes in Abu Dhabi. It also saw Barcelona earn another record by lifting their sixth trophy in 2009 – winning every competition they entered.

March 10, 2007
Scores first senior hat-trick for club at age 19 and does it in style against Barcelona's arch-rivals Real Madrid at the Nou Camp. All of Messi's goals were equalisers with the final one coming in the last minute and earning Barcelona, who were down to 10 men, a 3-3 draw.

May 27, 2009
Messi's header against Manchester United helped Barcelona win the Champions League title and in the process secure their first-ever treble, having already won the league and cup titles that season.

March 20, 2012
Becomes Barcelona's all-time leading goalscorer after scoring twice in the Primera Division match with Granada. Messi's second goal in the match saw him move on to 233 official goals, one more than the previous record set by Cesar Rodriguez during the 1940s and 50s.

Oct 16, 2004
Appears in first official match for Barcelona in the 1-0 derby win over Espanyol. At the age of 17 years, three months and 22 days, Messi becomes the second-youngest player to play a league game for Barcelona's first team.

Feb 16, 2013
Scores his 300th official goal for Barcelona in 2-1 win at Granada. Messi needed just 366 matches to achieve the feat.

March 17 2013
Handed Barcelona captaincy for the first time in an official match after Andres Iniesta was substituted against Rayo Vallecano.

OLYMPIC GOLD

Messi's greatest international achievement to date came in 2008 when he helped lead Argentina to the gold medal at the Beijing Olympic Games.

Messi's chance to be involved in Beijing was in doubt right up until his nation's opening game of the tournament. The day before, Barcelona won a court battle against FIFA, who insisted that clubs must release players under the age of 23 for the Games.

That meant Barcelona could stop Messi playing but he was picked to start for Argentina against the Ivory Coast and swept home the opening goal just before half-time before setting up Lautaro Acosta's late winner in a 2-1 triumph. It was only after the match that it was revealed Messi had asked to stay at the Olympics in a chat with Barcelona's new coach Pep Guardiola, who allowed the 21-year-old to stay in China and compete for his country.

Messi failed to find the net in the subsequent 1-0 win over Australia and, with Argentina safely through to the quarter-finals, he was left on the bench for a 2-0 victory over Serbia.

But, as at the Under-20 World Cup three years earlier, he had already shown the kind of skills that were capturing the imagination of the football world amid a talented Argentina side boasting the likes of Pablo Zabaleta, Juan Riquelme, Javier Mascherano, Sergio Aguero and Angel Di Maria.

Holland were the opposition in the quarter-finals and Messi was again on the scoresheet, charging down a loose ball before bursting through on the edge of the penalty area and going round the keeper to score.

Great through-ball

The match went to extra time though, before Messi was involved in the winner as he set up Di Maria with a great through-ball to clinch a tough 2-1 victory.

As in 2005, Brazil and Nigeria stood in the way of success, but their great South American rivals – led by recently-departed Barca team-mate Ronaldinho – proved little test in the semi-finals as Argentina easily triumphed 3-0.

Messi, in arguably the biggest game of his international career, did not disappoint in the Olympic final against Nigeria, capping a fine individual display with the pass for Di Maria's match-winning second-half chip.

Argentina had successfully defended their Olympic crown – and gold medallist Messi was the star of the show.

Messi consoles former Barcelona team-mate Ronaldinho, who was captain of Brazil, after the semi-final.

It's a golden moment as Messi (far left) dances on the top step of the podium in the Olympic medal ceremony and then kisses his precious gold medal.

Messi soaks up the atmosphere at the medal ceremony in Beijing.

OFF DUTY

Messi is all-action on the pitch and rarely misses a match, but the superstar knows how to relax when he does get some time off from football.

Messi and girlfriend Antonella are all dressed for team-mate Andres Iniesta's wedding at a Spanish castle.

With a statue of boot manufacturer adidas founder Adi Dassler.

Messi shows he is as speedy on a jetski as he is on the pitch as he takes Antonella for a spin.

Soaking up the sun with Antonella on a flash yacht off Ibiza, and with his new Audi Q7 club car in Barcelona.

EUROSTAR

Barcelona had only won one European Cup title in their history – against Sampdoria at Wembley back in 1992 – before Messi's arrival at the Nou Camp, but that statistic was soon about to change.

The first of the three Champions League winner's medals Messi has won so far came in 2006. Despite still being a teenager, he was a regular in Barcelona's team for the early part of the tournament and scored against Greek side Panathinaikos in the group stages.

However, he suffered a thigh injury during the quarter-final against Chelsea and was deemed unfit to play in the final, where Barcelona beat another English side, Arsenal, 2-1 in Paris.

Messi was bitterly disappointed not to have been involved in that game but he got another chance in 2009 after helping Barcelona reach the final again, and he was determined not to waste the opportunity.

Messi scored nine goals in the competition that season but his most important by far was his header in the final which sealed a 2-0 victory over Manchester United in Rome.

Barcelona were knocked out at the semi-final stage the following year, losing to eventual winners Inter Milan, but the Nou Camp club did not have to wait much longer to get their hands on the trophy again as

Messi earned his third winner's medal in 2011 – and Manchester United were again the victims.

Messi netted in every round, including both goals as Barcelona beat rivals Real Madrid 2-0 away from home in the semi-finals, and he was again on the scoresheet in the final as his side triumphed 3-1 over United at Wembley.

Dumped out

Messi was unable to inspire another Champions League final appearance in either 2012 or 2013 as Barcelona were dumped out in the semi-finals first by Chelsea and then by Bayern Munich. But he should have plenty of opportunities in the future to add to his medal tally.

The striker is also well on course to become the leading scorer in the history of the Champions League, having already passed 50 goals.

Barcelona fans let Messi go to their heads as they arrive at Wembley Stadium for the 2011 Champions League final against Manchester United.

"I think it will take us a long time to realise what we have achieved. To score in a Champions League final and win the league is unbelievable."

Manchester United goalkeeper Edwin van der Sar looks horrified as little Messi gets up to head the second goal in the 2009 final.

Back home in Barcelona, Messi gets in the party mood with his victorious Barca team-mates.

"Lionel is the best player I've ever seen, probably the best ever. He made the difference. Messi is unique, a one-off."

– Pep Guardiola after the 2011 final

CHAMPION AGAIN

Messi was on target again when Barcelona and Manchester United came face to face once more in the 2011 Champions League final, this time at Wembley. He got one of the goals in Barca's 3-1 victory – and celebrated in typical fashion.

EXPERT VIEW

Messi has enthralled and amazed football fans all over the world with his silky skills and awesome ability, but he has also made a huge impression on his fellow professionals. Here's what they say about him:

Tito Vilanova
Barcelona coach

"We do not know his limits. You should see how he trains every day – that urge he has to keep getting better. I think we will never see another player like this. He is the best in the world by far."

Samuel Eto'o
Cameroon striker and Barcelona team-mate between 2004 and 2009

"Messi is a God – as a person and even more so as a player. I hope that he wins the World Cup with Argentina. To the Gods of the world, all I ask is that you give him that chance."

Juan Sebastian Veron
Former Manchester United, Chelsea and Argentina midfield star

"Every time he grabs the ball and accelerates, I see Maradona. We must protect him. I'd personally put him in a drawer of my bedside table."

David Villa
Barcelona team-mate and Spain's all-time leading scorer

"He is doing incredible things. Each day he surprises everyone with a new record, he continually outdoes himself. Nobody can compare with him."

Messi with strike partners Samuel Eto'o and David Villa.

Ossie Ardiles
Former Spurs and Argentina midfield star

"For some time I thought Diego Maradona could never be surpassed, and nor could Pele, but no longer. I would now say that Lionel Messi will go down in history as the number one player of all time, the best that there ever was."

Ronaldo
Former Barcelona and Brazil striker, and world player of the year in 1996, 1997 and 2002

"He has so much creativity, he enchants us. And despite the fact that he's Argentinian, the great rivals of Brazil, he's a player who I admire a great deal. He is the best in the world, so far ahead of the rest. I wish I was 10 years younger so I could play with Messi."

Arsene Wenger
Arsenal manager, against whose team Messi scored all four goals in a 4-1 Champions League victory in 2010

"Messi is like a PlayStation player. He can punish any mistake, make a difference at any moment."

Three-time world player of the year Ronaldo and UEFA president Michel Platini hand Messi his third Ballon d'Or. Messi would go on to surpass Ronaldo by winning his fourth in January 2013.

Jupp Heynckes
Former Real Madrid and three-times Bayern Munich coach
"He is a phenomenon. He is in the league of Zinedine Zidane, Diego Maradona, Pele and Johan Cruyff. Anyone who scores 50 goals in a season is extra-terrestrial."

Michel Platini
UEFA president and former France star
"He's already a superb, fantastic player. You shouldn't try to place him in time. He's the great player of this generation, like there were great players in other generations."

Lucas Moura
Paris St Germain striker
"Messi is a genius, that says it all. I'm a big fan of Messi. He's the best player in the world right now and one of the best that I've seen play."

At the start of 2012, Messi was awarded FIFA's Ballon d'Or as world player of the year for the third time in a row.

A trademark lob over the goalkeeper was one of an incredible five goals scored against German team Bayer Leverkusen – the first player ever to strike that many in a Champions League game.

SIMPLY THE BEST

With all that Messi had achieved in his career already, it was hard to imagine that things could get any better or that he could do any more. But, incredibly, that was exactly what happened.

The year of 2012 may not have been the best for Barcelona, losing their Champions League and Primera Division titles and saying goodbye to Pep Guardiola, but it was a different story for Messi.

Not content to settle for what had gone before, Messi somehow found an extra gear and started re-writing the record books almost on a monthly basis. It started, as was becoming usual, with Messi being named the world's best player in FIFA's Ballon d'Or awards, winning the crown for the third successive year.

Then, after marking his 200th league appearance for Barcelona with four goals in a 5-1 win over Valencia, Messi scored his first hat-trick for Argentina in an international friendly win over Switzerland.

In March of 2012, Messi was celebrating two more amazing feats. He became the first player to score five times in a Champions League game as Barcelona thrashed Bayer Leverkusen 7-1. Then another Primera Division hat-trick, against Granada, saw him become Barcelona's all-time leading goalscorer in official games – at the age of just 24.

His second strike in that game saw him move on to 233 competitive goals for the club, one more than the previous record set by Cesar Rodriguez during the 1940s and 50s. Barca coach Guardiola said: "We are witnessing the best player in every sense. He does everything, and he does it every three days."

Messi was not finished there, though. Not by a

"My record stood for 40 years and now the best player in the world has broken it, and I'm delighted for him."

– Former West Germany striker Gerd Muller.

Messi celebrates his second goal against Granada in March 2012, which made him Barcelona's all-time record scorer – at the age of just 24.

long way. He scored all four goals in the 4-0 derby demolition of Espanyol in May to finish the 2011/12 Primera Division season with a staggering 50 goals.

That was the most in Spanish history and also the most by a player to win the European Golden Shoe as the top scorer in Europe.

The goals continued to fly in as the year progressed, including another Argentina hat-trick, this time against arch-rivals Brazil, as Messi raced his way towards another long-standing record.

An incredible player

That was broken on December 9 when two goals against Real Betis saw Messi beat former West Germany and Bayern Munich striker Gerd Muller's record of 85 goals in a calendar year that he achieved in 1972. Muller said: "My record stood for 40 years –

85 goals in 60 games – and now the best player in the world has broken it, and I'm delighted for him. He is an incredible player, gigantic."

Messi ended 2012 with 91 goals in all competitions for club and country, including nine hat-tricks, and the end of the year did not stop Messi's one-man attack on the record books either. His amazing exploits in 2012 inevitably saw him named as the best player in the world for the fourth successive time at the start of 2013 after again winning the FIFA Ballon d'Or – something nobody else has ever done.

On Messi went. He continued his red-hot form to claim another place in the history books by becoming the first player ever to score in consecutive Primera Division matches against every other team in the division after netting for the 19th successive league game in a 2-2 draw with Celta Vigo.

GREAT GOALS 2

Messi's career has been highlighted by loads of brilliant goals – some individual and some thanks to great teamwork. Here's a selection of the best:

Messi volleys into an empty net to complete his brilliant Champions League goal against Arsenal.

Messi celebrates after sliding his shot past Real Madrid defender Sergio Ramos.

BARCELONA 3 ARSENAL 1
Champions League, March 8, 2011

Many of Messi's best goals show just how good he is in all areas of the game. He can score many types of goal. Sometimes it is a mazy run, or a quick burst of pace or a powerful shot.

Messi gets much of the praise but it is easy to forget that he is actually a member of one of the best sides ever at Barcelona. His team-mates have also played big parts in many of Messi's goals, and one example of that was against Arsenal in a Champions League match at the Nou Camp.

The match was deep into injury time at the end of the first half when Andres Iniesta made the most of a mistake by Cesc Fabregas. Iniesta pinched the ball off the Arsenal midfielder and then produced a wonderful little pass to put Messi through inside the area. That was brilliant by Iniesta, but even better was to come from Messi. The Barcelona number 10 neatly controlled the ball before showing outrageous skill and confidence to loft the ball over Gunners keeper Manuel Almunia and volley into an empty net.

REAL MADRID 0 BARCELONA 2
Champions League, April 27, 2011

Messi has enjoyed some memorable matches against Barca's arch-rivals Real Madrid down the years, and this was another one as he scored both goals in a famous Champions League victory at the Bernabeu.

His second, in the 87th minute, was a wonderful individual goal. He evaded the attentions of four Madrid defenders as he raced into the penalty area before sliding a low right-footed shot past Iker Casillas.

Messi celebrates his cheeky free-kick against Atletico Madrid.

ATLETICO MADRID 1 BARCELONA 2
Primera Division, February 26, 2012

Messi is not only fantastic at dribbling and beating defenders, he is also pretty special from free-kicks.

One of his most memorable was against Atletico Madrid, when Messi showed both tremendous quick-thinking but also fantastic skill to earn Barcelona an 81st-minute winner at the Vicente Calderon.

Standing over a free-kick on the left corner of the penalty area, Messi spotted Atletico goalkeeper Thibaut Courtois still lining up his wall. The Argentinian took advantage to fire in a curling shot which found the top far right corner of the net with Courtois helpless.

GREAT MATES

Messi is always the centre of attention, but football is a team game, and he is part of possibly the greatest side ever to play the game.

While Messi has established himself as the world's top player, he admits he would not have achieved the success he has without the help of his team-mates.

He said: "I'm lucky that I get to play here at Barca and for Argentina, where I get to play with fantastic players. They have given me everything: the individual awards, the titles, the goals, everything. Without the help of my team-mates, I would be nothing."

A lot of those colleagues at Barcelona have played together for many years, having also graduated from the club's famous La Masia academy.

Cesc Fabregas and Gerard Pique both played alongside Messi in the youth ranks, while the likes of Andres Iniesta, Carles Puyol, Xavi, Victor Valdes and Sergio Busquets are all long-serving talents who have grown up learning the Barcelona philosophy.

That philosophy, which is bred into the players at La Masia and means that all levels of the club play football the same way, basically places more importance on the footballing ability of a kid rather than his size – and is why Messi was able to flourish.

Messi explained: "The Barca philosophy isn't about just one coach or another, it's based on an idea, a line that is laid down and all coaches follow. That has always been the way in which the club has worked with the academy."

Such has been the success of Barcelona's youth policy that eight of the players involved in their 2009 Champions League final win over Manchester United had all been at the club as youngsters.

That not only gives all those players a unique sense of commitment and loyalty to the club, it also means Barcelona's famous style of football is second nature and makes the team so effective.

Hugely successful

Messi said: "We've been playing together for a long time and we virtually know where the ball's going two or three passes in advance."

The same style of football has also been hugely successful for the Spanish national team, which is little surprise when lots of Barcelona players also play for their country.

Among them are Xavi, Iniesta, Puyol and Pique, who all helped Spain win the European Championships in 2008 and 2012 and the 2010 World Cup. Messi, of course does not play for Spain, but for Argentina. And without his Barcelona colleagues, the little star has not been quite as effective for his country, although that has started to change.

The three little geniuses that make Barcelona tick (from left), Messi, Andres Iniesta and Xavi.

"I'm lucky that I get to play here at Barca and for Argentina, where I get to play with fantastic players. They have given me everything."

Messi's childhood hero was Pablo Aimar, who starred for Argentina between 1999 and 2009. Aimar played in the number 10 position and was one of the most skilful players in the world. He started his career at River Plate before spells in Spain at Valencia and Real Zaragoza, and then moved to Portugal with Benfica.

June 2004
Following his move to Catalonia and with his super skills in Barcelona's youth teams attracting attention, Messi was offered the chance to play for Spain but turned it down in order to wait for the call from Argentina. He got it when he was picked in the Under-20 squad for a friendly against Paraguay.

August 17, 2005
Messi's debut for the senior Argentina team lasted less than 60 seconds! The 18-year-old wonderkid had just come on when his shirt was being pulled by Vilmos Vanczak. Messi threw his arm back and the defender went down holding his face. Messi was shown a red card and was soon in tears back in the dressing room.

A heartbroken Messi walks off after getting a red card within a minute of coming on for his international debut.

Messi celebrates scoring on his World Cup debut, Argentina's sixth goal against Serbia and Montenegro in 2006.

June 16, 2006
Messi stepped off the bench in the group game against Serbia and Montenegro to become the youngest ever Argentina player to appear at the World Cup, aged 18 years and 357 days. He then scored his nation's sixth goal in a 6-0 victory to ensure he is the sixth youngest player to ever score in the tournament.

July 3, 2010
Messi crashes out of his second World Cup still with just one goal to his name in two tournaments. His goal came against Serbia and Montenegro in 2006 but Argentina lost to hosts Germany in the quarter-finals. Four years later it was Germany again who knocked out Messi and his mates in South Africa.

March 22, 2013
Messi, fourth on Argentina's all-time list of scorers, found the net twice in a 3-0 win over Venezuela to move on to 32 goals – just two short of legend Diego Maradona's tally. Gabriel Batistuta leads the way with 56.

FAN-TASTIC!

As well as being hailed as the greatest footballer in the world, Messi is also one of the most recognisable, and is worshipped wherever he goes.

Whether it is with banners, crazy masks or face paint, Messi's fans will always show their love for the world's greatest player.

Argentina fans revel in their little master with artwork and posters.

NATIONAL HERO

Messi's career in international football with Argentina so far has been a story full of ups and downs – but maybe one day it will have a happy ending.

Compared to the success he has enjoyed with Barcelona, Messi has not managed to do the same with his country – but it could have been very different if he had not stayed loyal to Argentina.

Following his move to Barca and with his potential very clear, Messi was offered the chance to play for Spain but turned it down in order to wait for his chance with Argentina. He said: "I would have never chosen to play for Spain because I am Argentine."

He got his wish in June 2004 when he was named in Argentina's Under-20 squad for a friendly against Paraguay. His success at the 2005 Under-20 World Cup then saw him get his first call-up to the senior team against Hungary on August 17 at the age of 18.

It was a moment that he had been dreaming of for so long but it soon turned into a nightmare as the wonderkid was brought off the bench in the 63rd minute and shown a red card less than 60 seconds later – a sending-off which left Messi in tears back in the dressing room.

He made what he described as a "re-debut" a month later before being handed his first senior start against Peru, and then netting his first goal for his country in a friendly against Croatia in March 2006. Legend Diego Maradona labelled Messi as his true successor,

saying: "I have seen the player who will inherit my place in Argentine football and his name is Messi."

But Messi's memories of his first World Cup in 2006 and Copa America in 2007 would not be happy after two disappointing exits. The lows were soon replaced by the high of 2008 as Messi inspired his country to Olympic gold in Beijing, but further struggles at international level were not far away in the shape of the 2010 World Cup.

Another miserable Copa America followed in 2011, this time on home soil, as Argentina were once more beaten in the quarter-finals.

Accusations

Plenty of questions were being asked of Messi. The best player in the world had regularly turned on the style to spearhead Barcelona to glory but his own nation – a football-mad country starved of success in Brazil's shadow – had been left wanting.

Was Messi hindered by Argentina's style of play compared to Barca's? Or maybe it was a lack of quality around him compared to the likes of Xavi and Andres Iniesta at the Nou Camp?

Messi has always rejected accusations that he is more bothered about Barcelona and does not care about Argentina as much because he has lived in Spain for so long. He admits that hurts him and he is desperate to achieve success with Argentina.

There are signs that could change. New coach Alejandro Sabella handed Messi the captain's armband in August 2011, and has made the left-footed magician the focal point of his team.

Messi responded with stunning effect, finding the net a record-equalling 12 times in nine appearances in 2012. By May 2013, he was fourth in the country's all-time list of scorers with 32 goals – just two short of Maradona's total

Messi's international career may have been a bumpy ride to date, but he will ensure all of that is forgotten if he lifts the World Cup in Brazil in 2014.

Messi scored his first senior international goal, against Croatia in 2006.

New coach Alejandro Sabella made Messi captain of Argentina in 2011.

"I would have never chosen to play for Spain because I am Argentine."

THE WORLD STAGE

Many people believe Messi cannot truly be regarded as one of the all-time best players in football until he has helped his country win the World Cup.

For all of his success at Barcelona, Messi has struggled to wave his magic wand on the biggest stage of them all.

Having recovered from injury, Messi was first selected for World Cup duty in the Argentina squad which travelled to Germany in 2006.

After remaining unused for the opening group game, he stepped off the bench in the 75th minute against Serbia and Montenegro. That made him the youngest Argentinian ever to appear at the World Cup aged 18 years and 357 days.

Messi had already set up one goal when he bagged the last in a 6-0 rout to ensure he again wrote his name in the history books as the sixth youngest player to ever score at the tournament.

Yet disappointment was to follow for both Messi and Argentina in the quarter-finals as they crashed out of the competition to hosts Germany on penalties. Coach Jose Pekerman left Messi on the bench and was criticised for his negative tactics.

Further misery was to come four years later. After being handed the famous number 10 shirt by the legendary Diego Maradona in what was the first 2010 World Cup qualifier since his sensational appointment as coach, Messi bagged the opener in a comfortable 4-0 win over Venezuela.

But Argentina had a poor qualification campaign and, with Messi scoring only four times, they only scraped through to the tournament in South Africa.

Embarrassed

Matters did not improve much once there as, despite breezing through to the quarter-finals, Argentina were embarrassed 4-0 by Germany once again.

Messi had shown glimpses of his brilliance against the lesser teams during the group stages and second round but failed to score in all five matches, leaving him with two last-eight exits and just one single World Cup goal to his name across both tournaments.

The 2014 World Cup in Brazil provides one of arguably two remaining chances to really leave his mark at the highest level of the world game.

Messi celebrates after scoring Argentina's final goal in the 6-0 win over Serbia and Montenegro in his first World Cup appearance.

Messi's goal against Serbia and Montenegro in Germany in 2006 remains his only goal so far in a World Cup finals.

10 AND OUT

Messi scored against Venezuela in qualifying for the 2010 World Cup after being given the famous number 10 shirt for the first time by new coach Diego Maradona, but Argentina's trip to the finals in South Africa brought more misery.

They got through to the quarter-finals again, but once more Germany stood in their way and this time they powered to a 4-0 win to leave Messi and Argentina distraught.

Messi celebrates scoring against Venezuela in qualifying – his first game in the number 10 shirt for Argentina.

The 4-0 quarter-final defeat against Germany left Messi bitterly disappointed – and in need of a hug from coach Diego Maradona.

COACH PARTY

Messi has played under several coaches and managers during his club and international career and has not failed to impress any of them.

Pep Guardiola

Led Barcelona to an amazing period of success with 14 trophies in just four seasons and played a key role in helping Messi develop into the best player in the world.

"Like Michael Jordan in basketball, Messi is dominating his sport. Very few people in history have managed to dominate their sport the way Jordan and Messi have.

"I feel sorry for those who want to compete for Messi's throne – it's impossible, this kid is unique. He doesn't just score lots of goals, but he scores lots of great goals, each one being better than the last.

"The throne belongs to him, and no one else but him will decide when he vacates it. He's the best there is. There's no one else. I can count myself lucky to have been his coach."

Former Holland international star Frank Rijkaard was the Barcelona coach who gave Messi his first-team chance.

Frank Rijkaard

Gave Messi his Barcelona debut during his time in charge at the Nou Camp between 2003 and 2008.

"He's an incredible person. Messi is not simply a uniquely talented footballer. He's also strong mentally, very bright and exceptionally dedicated to his job.

"Personally speaking I enjoy watching him play and I'm deeply proud of him and what he has achieved. Quite simply, he's the best."

Messi with then Argentina coach Diego Maradona after the 4-1 win over South Korea at the 2010 World Cup in South Africa.

Diego Maradona

Argentina's coach between 2008 and 2010 and regarded by some as the best player in history, and to whom Messi is often compared.

"If you have a player as good as Leo, who is the best player in the world, I think it would be a sin not to give Messi to the people, to the team, and leave out the player who can certainly make the difference in a match."

"Cristiano Ronaldo is a great human footballer, but Messi is a Martian."

– Alfio Basile, Argentina coach 2006-2008

Alejandro Sabella

Former Sheffield United and Leeds midfielder who became Argentina coach in 2011 and made Messi captain.

"The control he has of the ball at full pace is amazing. It reminds me of the Scalextric I used to play as a kid – those cars going flat out from a standing start."

GLOBAL SUPERSTAR

Messi is now undeniably the best player in the modern game, and it has made him recognisable all over the world.

His obvious qualities on the pitch as well as his humble and gracious attitude have made Lionel Messi a role model for millions of fans.

The Argentinian has twice been included in *Time* magazine's famous annual list of the 100 most influential people in the world. In 2012 he was named as the third most marketable athlete, ahead of the likes of Usain Bolt and Cristiano Ronaldo. That means companies were all trying to get Messi to advertise their products and it led to big sponsorship deals with brands such as adidas, Pepsi and EA Sports (the creators of computer game FIFA 13).

In April 2011, Messi launched a Facebook page which two years later had over 45 million followers.

It has also been announced that a film about his life is due to be made and hopefully released in time for the 2014 World Cup.

Famous waxwork museum Madame Tussauds have already made a lifesize figure of the Barcelona forward which has been on display to visitors since September 2012. Messi's hometown of Rosario also plan to get in on the act by opening a sports museum mostly dedicated to their sporting hero by 2015.

Goodwill ambassador

Nicknamed 'the flea' due to his size, speed and balance, Messi has also been the subject of more wacky adulation including the pure gold replica of

A fan poses with the wax figure of Messi at the Madame Tussauds exhibition in Tokyo.

Messi's role as a goodwill ambassador for children's welfare organisation Unicef is important to him, and he often hosts children at the Nou Camp.

his magical left foot on sale in Japan.

Charity work forms a large part of Messi's life, especially helping out kids in need. It includes the Leo Messi Foundation he set up in 2007 to help vulnerable children and his role as a goodwill ambassador for Unicef.

Messi was also in the news in April 2013 when he sent newly elected Pope Francis, a fellow Argentinian and football fan, a signed Barcelona shirt which included the message "with much affection".

Despite his appeal, Messi is not as well known in the United States, where sports such as American football, basketball, baseball and ice hockey are more popular. By June 2012, Messi was 11th in the list of athletes earning the most money. If he can become more famous in the United States, he could soon be climbing that league table too.

GREAT GOALS 3

Domestic competition, Champions League or international football — it doesn't matter to Messi, who can score fantastic goals anywhere.

ARGENTINA 4 BRAZIL 3

International friendly, June 9, 2012

Does it get much better than this? Playing against your biggest rivals, five minutes to go, the game locked at 3-3 and if you score one more goal you complete your hat-trick and win the game.

Even a tap-in would have been a fairytale end to the game, but the wizard Messi conjured up something just a little more special.

Messi's first two goals in the game weren't bad, but his third and match-winner was simply brilliant. There appeared little danger as he was given the ball out wide near the halfway line, but he immediately skipped past a Brazil defender before racing full speed towards the penalty area.

Then, 25 yards out from goal, he unleashed an unstoppable left-footed thunderbolt which flew into the far top corner of the net with Brazil goalkeeper Rafael Barbosa rooted to the spot.

BARCELONA 4 REAL BETIS 2

Primera Division, May 5, 2013

Another perfect example of how Messi can score unforgettable team goals as well as individual goals was in the league match against Real Betis.

Barcelona were leading 3-2 when three of their forward players combined to devastating effect to add a fourth goal and seal the win.

Alexis Sanchez started the move with pass into Messi near the edge of the penalty box. Messi then played the ball on to Andres Iniesta, whose fantastic back-heel returned the ball to Alexis who had run into the area.

Alexis could have shot himself but he decided to play an inch-perfect pass across goal to Messi, who had got in behind the Betis defence to side-foot home at the far post.

Three players, eight seconds, nine touches, goal. Simply unstoppable.

Messi beats Brazil defender Juan to score his brilliant third goal and clinch a 4-3 win.

BARCELONA 4 AC MILAN 0

Champions League, March 12, 2013

Barcelona looked to be on their way out of the Champions League at the hands of AC Milan after losing the first leg 2-0 in Italy but Messi had other ideas. He started the fightback with a brilliant goal in the fifth minute of the second leg.

Six different players were involved as Barca moved the ball and looked to drag their opponents out of postion. Then, in the blink of an eye, the ball was in the back of the net as Messi played a quick one-two with Xavi on the edge of the box before unleashing a superb curling shot into the top corner of the net. Messi scored again before half-time and Barcelona went on to win 4-0.

Messi celebrates with team-mates Dani Alves, Jordi Alba, David Villa and Andres Iniesta after scoring against AC Milan.

March 7 2012
Becomes the first player to score five goals in a Champions League game as Barcelona thrash Bayer Leverkusen 7-1.

May 12, 2012
Finishes the season with an incredible 50 goals in the league – a Primera Division record and also beating the previous-best mark to win the European Golden Shoe, which was the 47 goals scored by Romanian Dudu Georgescu for Dinamo Bucharest in 1976/77.

Dec 9, 2012
Breaks the record for the most goals in a calendar year with his double against Real Betis taking him to 86 in all competitions for Barcelona and Argentina, overtaking Bayern Munich and Germany legend Gerd Muller's record from 1972. Messi ended 2012 with a breathtaking 91 goals.

RECORD BREAKER

Jan 7, 2013
Becomes the first footballer to win FIFA's World Player of the Year/ Ballon d'Or award four times after being named the best player on the planet for the fourth successive year.

March 30, 2013
Messi becomes the first player in Primera Division history to score in consecutive matches against every other team in the division after netting for the 19th successive league game in the 2-2 draw with Celta Vigo.

March 9 2013
Scores in 17th Primera Division match on the trot – a record.

WHAT NEXT?

What does the future hold for Messi? What is there still to achieve for someone who had already done more by his mid-20s than most professional footballers have done in the history of the game?

There are still some significant records that are within Messi's sights and which could be broken in the coming years, including becoming the leading scorer in both the Primera Division and Champions League.

There is also his ambition to win the World Cup, to emulate what many of his Barcelona team-mates have done with Spain and what his hero Diego Maradona did with Argentina in 1986.

As for where he might play in the future, Messi has never shown any desire to leave Barcelona for another top European club. He said in 2012: "This is my home, my club. I owe everything to Barca. I'm very happy here."

However, he might yet decide to return to Argentina at some point and see out his final playing days in his homeland, some two decades after first leaving.

Once he does stop playing, Messi will be able to reflect properly on all the amazing things that have happened to him during his time in the game.

As he says: "I don't think it will be until after I've retired that I'm fully aware of what I've done or what I've achieved in my career."

There is one thing Messi is hoping to guarantee before he hangs up his boots though – that he is remembered by future generations for all the right reasons.

Spectacular goals

"I'm more concerned about being a good person than being the best footballer in the world," he said. "My hope is that when I retire that I'm remembered as a good guy."

But even if Messi does finish without breaking any more records or scoring any more spectacular goals, he has still already done more than enough to entertain millions of football fans, and then we can all bid him farewell and simply say: 'Lionel Andres Messi, thanks for the memories.'

Spectacular goals have given Messi's fans plenty of memories to treasure.

"This is my home, my club. I owe everything to Barca. I'm very happy here."

KNOW YOUR STUFF

Here are 20 questions to test your Messi knowledge. All of the answers can be found somewhere in the book!

1 What is Messi's middle name?

2 In which Argentinian city was Messi born?

3 Against which team did Messi score five goals in a single Champions League match in 2012?

4 Which of the following players has played alongside Messi for Argentina: Zlatan Ibrahimovic, Angel Di Maria or David Villa?

5 At what age did Messi score his first competitive goal for Barcelona in 2005?

6 Who were the same opponents in the final when Barcelona won the 2009 and 2011 Champions League titles?

7 Name Messi's first two first-team managers at Barcelona?

8 What date is Messi's birthday?

9 Messi beat the record of which former Germany striker when he scored 91 goals in 2012?

10 How many league goals did Messi score during the 2011/12 season?

11 Against which team did Messi make his first-team debut with Barcelona?

12 Which other country could Messi have played for, other than Argentina?

13 Who was Barcelona's leading all-time scorer before Messi broke his record in 2012 and how many goals did that player score for the club?

14 How many European Cups had Barcelona won before Messi joined the club?

15 Which six trophies did Barcelona win in the same year in 2009?

16 How many goals did Messi score on his 200th league appearance for Barcelona?

17 What number shirt does Messi normally wear?

18 Against which team did Messi first captain Barcelona in an official match?

19 Who did Messi make his full Argentina debut against in 2005?

20 What is Messi's nickname?

It's tough work being a superstar – Messi takes a break during training with Argentina.